NOTES

DATE _____ TIME _____ ⭕ HOME ⭕ AWAY

OPPONENTS _____ FINAL SCORE _____ : _____

NO.	PLAYERS	RATING	MIN.PLAYED	NOTES

DIAGRAM

KEY POINTS

MATCH
CLIPBOARD

SUBSTITUTIONS

TEAM GOALS

BEST PERFORMANCE

NOTES

DATE _____ TIME _____   ◯ HOME   ◯ AWAY

OPPONENTS _____   FINAL SCORE _____:_____

NO.	PLAYERS	RATING	MIN.PLAYED	NOTES

DIAGRAM

KEY POINTS

MATCH
CLIPBOARD

SUBSTITUTIONS

TEAM GOALS

BEST PERFORMANCE

NOTES

DATE _____ TIME _____   ◯ HOME   ◯ AWAY

OPPONENTS _____   FINAL SCORE _____ : _____

NO.	PLAYERS	RATING	MIN.PLAYED	NOTES

DIAGRAM

KEY POINTS

MATCH
CLIPBOARD

SUBSTITUTIONS

TEAM GOALS

BEST PERFORMANCE

NOTES

DATE _____ TIME _____ ◯ HOME ◯ AWAY

OPPONENTS _____ FINAL SCORE _____:___

NO.	PLAYERS	RATING	MIN.PLAYED	NOTES

DIAGRAM

KEY POINTS

MATCH CLIPBOARD

SUBSTITUTIONS

TEAM GOALS

BEST PERFORMANCE

NOTES

DATE _____ TIME _____ ◯ HOME ◯ AWAY

OPPONENTS _____ FINAL SCORE _____ : _____

NO.	PLAYERS	RATING	MIN.PLAYED	NOTES

DIAGRAM

KEY POINTS

MATCH
CLIPBOARD

SUBSTITUTIONS

TEAM GOALS

BEST PERFORMANCE

NOTES

DATE _____ TIME _____ ◯ HOME ◯ AWAY

OPPONENTS _____ FINAL SCORE _____:_____

NO.	PLAYERS	RATING	MIN. PLAYED	NOTES

DIAGRAM

KEY POINTS

MATCH CLIPBOARD

SUBSTITUTIONS

TEAM GOALS

BEST PERFORMANCE

NOTES

DATE _____ TIME _____   ◯ HOME   ◯ AWAY

OPPONENTS _____   FINAL SCORE _____ : _____

NO.	PLAYERS	RATING	MIN.PLAYED	NOTES

DIAGRAM

KEY POINTS

MATCH CLIPBOARD

SUBSTITUTIONS

TEAM GOALS

BEST PERFORMANCE

NOTES

DATE _____ TIME _____ ◯ HOME ◯ AWAY

OPPONENTS _____ FINAL SCORE _____ : _____

NO.	PLAYERS	RATING	MIN.PLAYED	NOTES

DIAGRAM

KEY POINTS

MATCH CLIPBOARD

SUBSTITUTIONS

TEAM GOALS

BEST PERFORMANCE

NOTES

DATE _____   TIME _____   ◯ HOME   ◯ AWAY

OPPONENTS _____   FINAL SCORE _____ :_____

NO.	PLAYERS	RATING	MIN.PLAYED	NOTES

DIAGRAM

KEY POINTS

MATCH
CLIPBOARD

SUBSTITUTIONS

TEAM GOALS

BEST PERFORMANCE

NOTES

DATE _____ TIME _____ ◯ HOME ◯ AWAY

OPPONENTS _____ FINAL SCORE _____ : _____

NO.	PLAYERS	RATING	MIN.PLAYED	NOTES

DIAGRAM

KEY POINTS

MATCH
CLIPBOARD

SUBSTITUTIONS

TEAM GOALS

BEST PERFORMANCE

NOTES

DATE _____   TIME _____   ◯ HOME   ◯ AWAY

OPPONENTS _____   FINAL SCORE _____ : _____

NO.	PLAYERS	RATING	MIN.PLAYED	NOTES

DIAGRAM

KEY POINTS

MATCH CLIPBOARD

SUBSTITUTIONS

TEAM GOALS

BEST PERFORMANCE

NOTES

DATE _____ TIME _____ ○ HOME ○ AWAY

OPPONENTS _____ FINAL SCORE _____ : _____

NO.	PLAYERS	RATING	MIN.PLAYED	NOTES

DIAGRAM

KEY POINTS

MATCH CLIPBOARD

SUBSTITUTIONS

TEAM GOALS

BEST PERFORMANCE

NOTES

DATE _____ TIME _____ ◯ HOME ◯ AWAY

OPPONENTS _____ FINAL SCORE _____ : _____

NO.	PLAYERS	RATING	MIN.PLAYED	NOTES

DIAGRAM

KEY POINTS

MATCH
CLIPBOARD

SUBSTITUTIONS

TEAM GOALS

BEST PERFORMANCE

NOTES

DATE _____ TIME _____ ◯ HOME ◯ AWAY

OPPONENTS _____ FINAL SCORE _____ :

NO.	PLAYERS	RATING	MIN.PLAYED	NOTES

DIAGRAM

KEY POINTS

MATCH CLIPBOARD

SUBSTITUTIONS

TEAM GOALS

BEST PERFORMANCE

NOTES

DATE _____ TIME _____ ◯ HOME ◯ AWAY

OPPONENTS _____ FINAL SCORE _____ :

NO.	PLAYERS	RATING	MIN.PLAYED	NOTES

DIAGRAM

KEY POINTS

MATCH
CLIPBOARD

SUBSTITUTIONS

TEAM GOALS

BEST PERFORMANCE

NOTES

DATE _____ TIME _____ ◯ HOME ◯ AWAY

OPPONENTS _____ FINAL SCORE _____ :

NO.	PLAYERS	RATING	MIN.PLAYED	NOTES

DIAGRAM

KEY POINTS

MATCH CLIPBOARD

SUBSTITUTIONS

TEAM GOALS

BEST PERFORMANCE

NOTES

DATE _____   TIME _____   ◯ HOME   ◯ AWAY

OPPONENTS _____   FINAL SCORE _____ : _____

NO.	PLAYERS	RATING	MIN.PLAYED	NOTES

DIAGRAM

KEY POINTS

MATCH
CLIPBOARD

SUBSTITUTIONS

TEAM GOALS

BEST PERFORMANCE

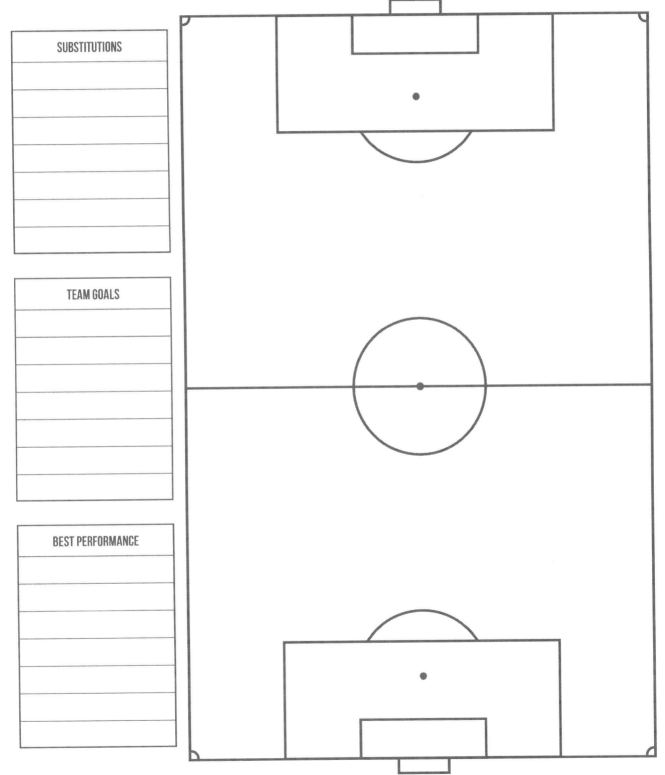

NOTES

DATE _____ TIME _____   ◯ HOME   ◯ AWAY

OPPONENTS _____   FINAL SCORE _____ : _____

NO.	PLAYERS	RATING	MIN.PLAYED	NOTES

DIAGRAM

KEY POINTS

MATCH CLIPBOARD

SUBSTITUTIONS

TEAM GOALS

BEST PERFORMANCE

NOTES

DATE _____ TIME _____ ◯ HOME ◯ AWAY

OPPONENTS _____ FINAL SCORE _____ : _____

NO.	PLAYERS	RATING	MIN.PLAYED	NOTES

DIAGRAM

KEY POINTS

MATCH CLIPBOARD

SUBSTITUTIONS

TEAM GOALS

BEST PERFORMANCE

NOTES

DATE _____ TIME _____ ◯ HOME ◯ AWAY

OPPONENTS _____ FINAL SCORE _____ :

NO.	PLAYERS	RATING	MIN.PLAYED	NOTES

DIAGRAM

KEY POINTS

MATCH CLIPBOARD

SUBSTITUTIONS

TEAM GOALS

BEST PERFORMANCE

NOTES

DATE _____ TIME _____ ⬭ HOME ⬭ AWAY

OPPONENTS _____ FINAL SCORE _____ : _____

NO.	PLAYERS	RATING	MIN.PLAYED	NOTES

DIAGRAM

KEY POINTS

MATCH
CLIPBOARD

SUBSTITUTIONS

TEAM GOALS

BEST PERFORMANCE

NOTES

DATE _____ TIME _____ ◯ HOME ◯ AWAY

OPPONENTS _____ FINAL SCORE _____ :

NO.	PLAYERS	RATING	MIN.PLAYED	NOTES

DIAGRAM

KEY POINTS

MATCH CLIPBOARD

SUBSTITUTIONS

TEAM GOALS

BEST PERFORMANCE

NOTES

DATE _____ TIME _____ ◯ HOME ◯ AWAY

OPPONENTS _____ FINAL SCORE _____ : _____

NO.	PLAYERS	RATING	MIN.PLAYED	NOTES

DIAGRAM

KEY POINTS

MATCH
CLIPBOARD

SUBSTITUTIONS

TEAM GOALS

BEST PERFORMANCE

NOTES

DATE _____ TIME _____   ◯ HOME   ◯ AWAY

OPPONENTS _____   FINAL SCORE _____ : _____

NO.	PLAYERS	RATING	MIN.PLAYED	NOTES

DIAGRAM

KEY POINTS

MATCH
CLIPBOARD

SUBSTITUTIONS

TEAM GOALS

BEST PERFORMANCE

NOTES

DATE _____ TIME _____ ◯ HOME ◯ AWAY

OPPONENTS _____ FINAL SCORE _____ : _____

NO.	PLAYERS	RATING	MIN.PLAYED	NOTES

DIAGRAM

KEY POINTS

MATCH CLIPBOARD

SUBSTITUTIONS

TEAM GOALS

BEST PERFORMANCE

NOTES

DATE _____ TIME _____ ◯ HOME ◯ AWAY

OPPONENTS _____ FINAL SCORE _____ : _____

NO.	PLAYERS	RATING	MIN.PLAYED	NOTES

DIAGRAM

KEY POINTS

MATCH CLIPBOARD

SUBSTITUTIONS

TEAM GOALS

BEST PERFORMANCE

NOTES

DATE _____ TIME _____   ◯ HOME   ◯ AWAY

OPPONENTS _____   FINAL SCORE _____ : _____

NO.	PLAYERS	RATING	MIN.PLAYED	NOTES

DIAGRAM

KEY POINTS

MATCH
CLIPBOARD

SUBSTITUTIONS

TEAM GOALS

BEST PERFORMANCE

NOTES

DATE _____ TIME _____ ◯ HOME ◯ AWAY

OPPONENTS _____ FINAL SCORE _____ : _____

NO.	PLAYERS	RATING	MIN.PLAYED	NOTES

DIAGRAM

KEY POINTS

MATCH CLIPBOARD

SUBSTITUTIONS

TEAM GOALS

BEST PERFORMANCE

NOTES

DATE _____ TIME _____   ◯ HOME   ◯ AWAY

OPPONENTS _____   FINAL SCORE _____ :

NO.	PLAYERS	RATING	MIN.PLAYED	NOTES

DIAGRAM

KEY POINTS

MATCH
CLIPBOARD

SUBSTITUTIONS

TEAM GOALS

BEST PERFORMANCE

NOTES

DATE _____ TIME _____ ○ HOME ○ AWAY

OPPONENTS _____ FINAL SCORE _____ : _____

NO.	PLAYERS	RATING	MIN.PLAYED	NOTES

DIAGRAM

KEY POINTS

MATCH CLIPBOARD

SUBSTITUTIONS

TEAM GOALS

BEST PERFORMANCE

NOTES

DATE _____ TIME _____ ◯ HOME ◯ AWAY

OPPONENTS _____ FINAL SCORE _____ : _____

NO.	PLAYERS	RATING	MIN.PLAYED	NOTES

DIAGRAM

KEY POINTS

MATCH
CLIPBOARD

SUBSTITUTIONS

TEAM GOALS

BEST PERFORMANCE

NOTES

DATE _____ TIME _____ ◯ HOME ◯ AWAY

OPPONENTS _____ FINAL SCORE _____ : _____

NO.	PLAYERS	RATING	MIN.PLAYED	NOTES

DIAGRAM

KEY POINTS

MATCH
CLIPBOARD

SUBSTITUTIONS

TEAM GOALS

BEST PERFORMANCE

NOTES

DATE _____ TIME _____   ◯ HOME   ◯ AWAY

OPPONENTS _____   FINAL SCORE _____ : _____

NO.	PLAYERS	RATING	MIN.PLAYED	NOTES

DIAGRAM

KEY POINTS

MATCH
CLIPBOARD

SUBSTITUTIONS

TEAM GOALS

BEST PERFORMANCE

NOTES

DATE _____ TIME _____ ◯ HOME ◯ AWAY

OPPONENTS _____ FINAL SCORE _____ :

NO.	PLAYERS	RATING	MIN.PLAYED	NOTES

DIAGRAM

KEY POINTS

MATCH CLIPBOARD

SUBSTITUTIONS

TEAM GOALS

BEST PERFORMANCE

NOTES

DATE _____ TIME _____   ◯ HOME   ◯ AWAY

OPPONENTS _____   FINAL SCORE _____ : _____

NO.	PLAYERS	RATING	MIN.PLAYED	NOTES

DIAGRAM

KEY POINTS

MATCH
CLIPBOARD

TEAM GOALS

BEST PERFORMANCE

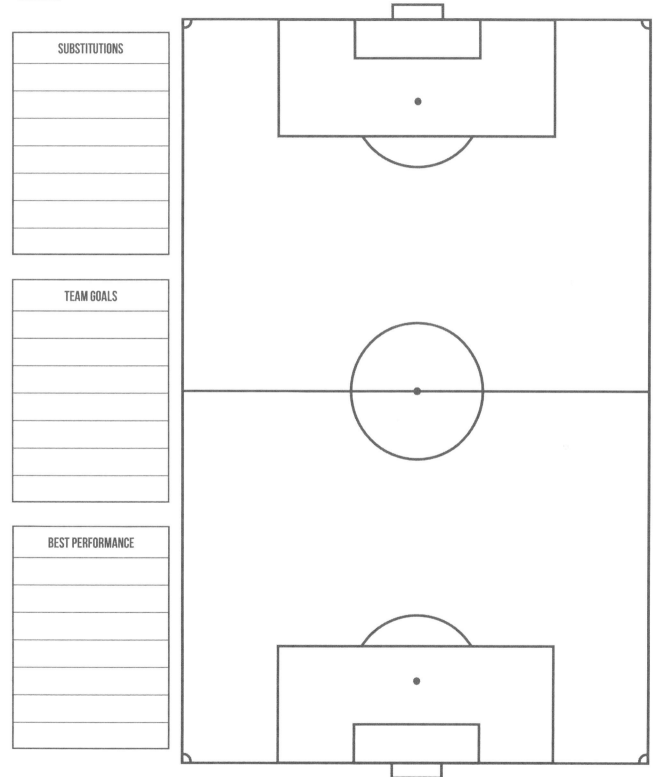

NOTES

DATE _____ TIME _____ ◯ HOME ◯ AWAY

OPPONENTS _____ FINAL SCORE _____ : _____

NO.	PLAYERS	RATING	MIN.PLAYED	NOTES

DIAGRAM

KEY POINTS

MATCH CLIPBOARD

SUBSTITUTIONS

TEAM GOALS

BEST PERFORMANCE

NOTES

DATE _____ TIME _____ ◯ HOME ◯ AWAY

OPPONENTS _____ FINAL SCORE _____ : _____

NO.	PLAYERS	RATING	MIN.PLAYED	NOTES

DIAGRAM

KEY POINTS

MATCH
CLIPBOARD

SUBSTITUTIONS

TEAM GOALS

BEST PERFORMANCE

NOTES

DATE _____ TIME _____   ◯ HOME ◯ AWAY

OPPONENTS _____   FINAL SCORE _____ : _____

NO.	PLAYERS	RATING	MIN.PLAYED	NOTES

DIAGRAM

KEY POINTS

MATCH CLIPBOARD

SUBSTITUTIONS

TEAM GOALS

BEST PERFORMANCE

NOTES

DATE _____ TIME _____ ◯ HOME ◯ AWAY

OPPONENTS _____ FINAL SCORE _____ : ....

NO.	PLAYERS	RATING	MIN.PLAYED	NOTES

DIAGRAM

KEY POINTS

MATCH
CLIPBOARD

SUBSTITUTIONS

TEAM GOALS

BEST PERFORMANCE

NOTES

DATE _____ TIME _____ ◯ HOME ◯ AWAY

OPPONENTS _____ FINAL SCORE _____ : _____

NO.	PLAYERS	RATING	MIN.PLAYED	NOTES

DIAGRAM

KEY POINTS

MATCH
CLIPBOARD

SUBSTITUTIONS

TEAM GOALS

BEST PERFORMANCE

NOTES

DATE _____ TIME _____ ◯ HOME ◯ AWAY

OPPONENTS _____ FINAL SCORE _____ : _____

NO.	PLAYERS	RATING	MIN.PLAYED	NOTES

DIAGRAM

KEY POINTS

MATCH
CLIPBOARD

SUBSTITUTIONS

TEAM GOALS

BEST PERFORMANCE

NOTES

DATE _____ TIME _____ ◯ HOME ◯ AWAY

OPPONENTS _____ FINAL SCORE _____ : _____

NO.	PLAYERS	RATING	MIN.PLAYED	NOTES

DIAGRAM

KEY POINTS

MATCH
CLIPBOARD

SUBSTITUTIONS

TEAM GOALS

BEST PERFORMANCE

NOTES

Printed in Great Britain
by Amazon